REIKI HELPS YOU FEEL BETTER

A GUIDE FOR YOUNG PEOPLE AND CURIOUS ADULTS

Tiffany Hunter, PhD

Printed in the United States of America

First Edition 2020

ISBN: 978-0-578-79057-2 (Paperback)

Library of Congress Control Number: 2020919049

Cover Design by: Fiaz Ahmed – 99Designs.com/profiles/1735673
Interior Design by: Imran Shaikh – 99Designs.com/profiles/retina99
Illustrations by: Imran Shaikh – 99Designs.com/profiles/retina99
Author Photo: Deborah Tarrant

Published by: Healing for People Press, San Francisco, California

www.HealingforPeople.com

DEDICATION

For Maya and Liam. Thank you for making me a Tama.
It means the world to me.

THANK YOU

It's been my joy to create this book and I have many to thank.

To my students and clients of all ages, you are amazing, insightful, hilarious and full of courage. You inspire me to bring my best, redefine what 'best' is, then bring it all over again.

To Jim. Because this, like so many things, circles back to you, your strength, your willingness to share, and your unwavering belief in me.

To Claudia, Sue, Amelia and Cynthia. Wow, and double wow. Thank you for the depth of your belief in what I'm doing and the commitment to helping me do it. I am better for your presence and honored to be included in your team.

To Karen, for all the ways you inspire and nurture me. Thank you for lending me your considerable strength and incredible presence. You are extraordinary and my world is brighter and fuller with you in it.

To Chyna. You are willing to reach down into your depths and offer what's needed. I couldn't possibly ask for more or receive more. I am a better human walking around this planet because of you and for that you will always find me standing right next to you. Just turn your head.

To my husband Reggie. You offer me soil to grow, scaffolding to build confidence, and your light to see my blind spots. Which is to say, you offer me you. Which is to say, you offer me everything. Sharing your gaze I know that I am seen, that I am accepted and that I am deeply, deeply loved. Thank you.

CONTENTS

Warning, warning!

These sections are for the adults and they're REALLY boring! Well, I hope they're not boring for the adults. But if you aren't an adult, ignore all of this and go find the page with the hedgehog on it (because honestly, who doesn't like hedgehogs?).

~~~~~~

FOREWORD

I honestly can't think of anyone else who could have written this book this well. I can't think of anyone else who could have so thoughtfully crafted its complicated message with such clarity and depth. And I can't think of anyone else who could have written it to appeal to kids while not losing their parents in the process. Tiffany is remarkably good at speaking with people from different generations and with different backgrounds. It's just one of the reasons she's such an effective teacher and an extraordinary healer.

When my daughter Maya was five, she started asking repeatedly for a Reiki attunement. We gave it time because we wanted to be sure she wanted it for herself and not because it was something so many of her family members practiced. When she was seven, again, after much asking on her part, we agreed to her attunement. There was never any question as to who her teacher would be. Not only had Tiffany taught kids Reiki for years, she also knew how to keep kids engaged and curious while teaching. Engaged and curious is a difficult balance, but one Tiffany is wonderfully effective in maintaining. Maya was the youngest student, the eldest was twelve, with both boys and girls in the class. I'm told the eldest, now seventeen, still advocates for Reiki to other teenagers as a way to help themselves get through high school. The stories Tiffany tells of Maya's attunement class are among my favorite Maya stories.

When my son Liam was about five, he also started asking for a Reiki attunement. He not only saw his sister give herself Reiki when she fell and skinned her knee, but he also saw her give herself Reiki when she is getting ready for bed or felt grumpy. For the same reasons as Maya, we waited for Liam's attunement. Liam received his attunement in the afternoon one day after school. As I'm sure you have guessed by now, Tiffany was his teacher.

To optimize Liam's experience as well as the kids who were also waiting on an attunement, Tiffany assembled a class of boys who were close in age to Liam. She would center the course around Reiki, but it was also designed to support these very active, intelligent and shy boys in learning Reiki without becoming bored or going deep within their own shell. She was effective not only in teaching them all about Reiki, but she kept them all invested in the class throughout the class. To do that well, Tiffany had to be able to keep the information clear, direct and action-packed, which is difficult when you consider that Reiki is a subject about natural healing—but she did it.

Tiffany is also largely responsible for me teaching on Reiki and writing on it. She not only encouraged me to start working in the field, she also insisted I take what I knew about Reiki and expand on it by going into more advanced forms of healing in energy medicine. She has always been someone who has encouraged the best in others by showing them things about themselves they are often too close to see for themselves. She's done that for me, and over the many years that I have known and worked with Tiffany, I have seen her do that for so many others.

My hope is that you will find this book enriching and enhancing to your lifestyle. I expect that you will. I also expect that you will enjoy this book cover to cover and share it with others. What I know for sure is that if you and your family use Reiki every day, you will feel better and I believe everyone—e v e r y o n e—deserves that.

Chyna Honey, *Author of the books, Understanding Reiki: From Self-Care to Energy Medicine* and *Using Reiki: Practical Essays that Bring Reiki into Daily Practice.*

Nope!

This section is still for the adults, so if a lot of adult words are just not your thing, go find the hedgehog and meet me there. But if you are an adult, this section will tell you a little about Reiki and what this book is trying to do.

A NOTE FOR ADULTS

The motive for this book

There is much information out in the world about Reiki. While I find most of it well-meaning and enthusiastic, it has been hard to make it specifically relevant or useful in the everyday lives of the people I know and work with, especially young people.[1] It's just one reason I've met so many people who have taken a Reiki class, loved it at the time, but never kept up with it or could explain comfortably and meaningfully what Reiki is and what it does.

This is disappointing, because if Reiki is anything, it is useful, and it's useful in the most uncomplicated, practical, and unassuming way. I hope that this book offers information worthy of the profound positive impact Reiki has on our lives, while honoring its unpretentious and accessible simplicity.

---

1   Fantastic exceptions to this are *Understanding Reiki: From Self-care to Energy Medicine* and *Using Reiki: Practical Essays that Bring Reiki into Daily Practice,* both by Chyna Honey. These are the books I use for my Reiki adult classes.

How to use this book

This book is for people who want to find out if Reiki could help them and their family, or for those who know how to do Reiki but feel unsatisfied with the explanations they were given for what, where, how and why. And if you were given this book as an accompaniment to your or your family's class, lucky you!

There's information here about what Reiki is, human energy in general, energy health and how to take care of it. Hopefully, it will help to make it easy to include Reiki as part of your normal life.

But you will not know how to do Reiki by the time you finish reading this book; nobody can learn Reiki from a book. It must be done with a Reiki teacher, and it must be done in person. This is for the same reason why a book about hydration could not actually hydrate you. I can write a book about water—what it does, why it's important, how to drink it—but I can't actually hydrate you without you, your body, and some water in front of me.

I'm aware that this may be disappointing and frustrating, but the inconvenient truth (for both of us) is that there is a component to the teaching that requires the physical body of the student and the teacher in the same place at the same time. I will always do my best to answer questions and connect with you if you reach out to me, but having a local teacher that you can develop a more immediate relationship with is always best.

What is Reiki?

Reiki is a healing practice that helps people feel better. It is easy to do once you learn it and can be done without having to carve out time during the day (like meditation). You can even do it without others noticing. Reiki repairs the daily wear and tear in our energy that we, as humans, experience every day. Let's break that down and see what it actually means.

Most everyone knows that humans are made of a mind and a body, but not everyone thinks about humans also being made of energy. But we are. We know this from recording the frequencies of our heart or brain waves and what that tells us about our health. We know this from standing in "someone's space" and how that feels. We know this from being aware we are being stared at from across the room, even if we can't see who is doing the looking. We know this from being around exhausting people or places, even though there's no physical reason for feeling so drained.[2]

This is an important piece of self-understanding because it means that we can start to take care of our energy health along with the rest of us. Reiki is part of that by repairing the damage done to our energy through wear and tear. Repairing wear and tear is a regular part of our

---

2 I would like to acknowledge here that this may not be everyone's experience. Not everyone is energy sensitive any more than everyone can see colors. However, people without energy sensitivity are just as impacted by it as people who are more viscerally sensitive to it. In the same way that being color blind does not mean the color is not there, everyone will benefit from better energy health and Reiki, regardless of their energy sensitivity.

lives already: our clothes, our skin, our car—all of it requires regular attention for simply being used and existing. Without that care, larger problems occur, and things don't work as well or feel as well. This is true whether it's brushing our teeth, putting oil in our car, or cleaning the kitchen counter. Most people have much more experience and information to be successful in taking care of wear and tear in the areas of our life involving our physical objects, our body and even our mental state, but not so much when it comes to taking care of our energy health.

The consequences of not taking care of our energy do not differ from any other sphere of our lives. We know that the consequences of not flossing our teeth or getting enough "down time" won't show up immediately. But over time, day after day, not repairing the damage of wear and tear means problems will show up; it's just a matter of time. Reiki is the remedy for this in the realm of our energy health. It's simple to learn, easy to use, and supremely accessible.

Thank you

If you are coming to this information as an adult, that's both daunting and amazing. You have a similar journey ahead of you as when you were just learning the importance of staying hydrated or brushing your teeth. But take heart—for most people, learning Reiki is easily done, and making it part of everyday life feels wonderful.

If you are thinking of getting this book for a young person, I congratulate you. You are giving them a start to understanding themselves as a whole being, to gain the opportunity to take care of themselves and the chance to feel better every day. What better gift to give the next generation than the ability to navigate their life and our world with more awareness and control?

Tiffany Hunter, PhD

INTRODUCTION

Welcome

Hi, welcome and nice to meet you. My name is Tiffany. I am not a hedgehog, but I am a Reiki teacher and I wrote this book. It's a book about how to feel better. It explains how to feel better by using Reiki. When you say the word Reiki out loud, it sounds like you're saying "ray-key" except there's no pause, it's just one word, Reiki. One word, two syllables.

Knowing about Reiki makes my life a lot easier. I feel less upset and sleep better. When my body hurts or I feel sick, Reiki helps with the pain. Reiki also makes it easier for me to think or pay attention to things. But the most wonderful way that Reiki helps me is to help me feel relaxed and calm. Reiki doesn't just help me. It helps millions of people all over the planet, including my own family. I hope you learn Reiki so it can help you, too. I wrote this book to give you the information you need to understand it.

Having a Reiki teacher

This book will tell you lots and lots of things, but you will need to have a Reiki teacher as well. Reading a book can't teach you Reiki for the same reason reading a book can't teach you to ride a bike. You can learn ABOUT riding a bike from a book, but to actually ride one, you need to go DO it. Reiki is the same, and to DO Reiki, you need a teacher. If you have one, that's great! Then your teacher and this book will be everything you need. If you don't have one, do not worry, they are easy to find. The person who gave you this book can help you, or you can ask another adult. Reiki teachers are not hiding and will be happy to meet you. While you are waiting to find your teacher, reading this book will start helping you, too. When you find your teacher, you will be able to do Reiki yourself.

Things to think about

At the end of every chapter is a section called Things to Think About (when I wrote that it sounded very loud, slow and with lots of echoes in my head:

THINGS TO THINK ABOUT!). Here you'll find things, as you might imagine, to think about: ideas, questions, conundrums and similar. There's no right or wrong answer to these questions. You get to decide for yourself what you think, and other people get to decide for themselves what they think. You can share your thoughts with others, or you can keep them private. That's up to you.

Things to think about

So, let's get on with it. Starting with the question ... what the heck IS Reiki?

CHAPTER ONE: WHAT IS REIKI?

Reiki is an energy vibration

Reiki is a bunch of things, depending on how you look at it. Most things are like that. A hedgehog (hey, I like hedgehogs, okay?) can

be described as an animal, as pointy, as a hibernator and as a snail eater. It's all still a hedgehog. I can describe Reiki as an energy vibration, as self-care, and as a club. Let's go through each one of those.

What is Reiki? Reiki is an energy vibration. Even if you don't know the word "vibration," you already know about them. Whenever you make a sound, you are making vibrations. If you touch the front of your throat while you hum, you can feel the vibration of your hum. You can feel the vibration in your body, even though you can't see it. Try it. Hummmmmmmm. You can't see it, but it's a vibration you can feel in

your body. Reiki is the same.

You also know about energy already. Scientists often define energy as the ability to get work done, or the ability to make a change. For example, kinetic energy is a type of energy, and it's the energy that transfers from your foot to a soccer ball when you kick it. The harder you kick the ball, the more kinetic energy transfers from your foot to the ball, and the further the ball goes. (Kinetic energy can't help you with the ball actually going into the goal, though—that's up to you!)

You can't see, hear or touch the energy transferring from your foot to the ball, but you can see what happens to the ball when the energy gets to it (even if it misses the goal). You won't be able to see the Reiki going into your body, but you will feel your body relax and feel better when it gets there.

So, Reiki is a vibration of energy that gets work done. You can't see the vibration, but you can feel it in your body, and it makes you feel better.

Reiki is self-care

What else is Reiki? Reiki is self-care. Have you ever heard that word before, self-care? You may not know that word

either, but you are already doing it. Self-care is taking care of yourself. You take care of yourself already by washing your hair and eating good food. You're also doing self-care when you get cozy or brush your teeth.

Reiki is self-care because it is a way to take care of yourself and help yourself feel better. Self-care is very important. There are different kinds of self-care; some self-care takes care of your body, like taking a shower; some takes care of your clothes, like getting them washed.

Can you imagine what would happen if you didn't do self-care? Without self-care, you could become ill or injured. You would certainly be very dirty.

This doesn't mean Reiki is just for you. You're allowed to use your Reiki on other people. It could help them, too! But mostly, you do it to yourself to take care of yourself, because when you do, you feel good. Taking care of yourself with Reiki helps you feel better.

Reiki is a club

When you learn Reiki, you'll have a teacher, and you'll meet the other people who are learning it, too. If you want to, you and those people can be a group together. Reiki connects people together, and if they want to, they can become like a team or a club.

And just like different schools have different volleyball teams, and those teams have different uniforms or rules about when practice starts, different groups of Reiki people may have different ideas about Reiki. You may meet people who

learned their Reiki somewhere else, and they may do things differently than how you and your teacher do them. It doesn't make you or them wrong, just different.

Whatever rules, ideas, habits, or traditions these different Reiki groups have, it doesn't actually matter to the energy vibration we call Reiki. Reiki, the energy vibration, doesn't change because of what people say or think about it. Reiki stays the same.

ICYMI

ICYMI means "In Case You Missed It". Just in case you didn't know that! (Uh, would that be JICYDKT?)

So, Reiki is a few things. It's a vibration. You may not see it, or smell it, but you can feel it in your body as you're doing it. It's something you do to take care of yourself, and we call that self-care.

It's also energy because it DOES something. In this case, it helps you feel better.

And lastly, Reiki is a kind of club because people learn it together and sometimes get together to have fun and learn more. But you don't have to do that if you don't want to.

But the most important thing is that Reiki won't notice or care if you remember any of those things I just said. It just works. Every time you use it, it'll help you.

Things to think about

1. What do you think is the difference between things you can learn from a book and things you can't? Which do you prefer?

2. Is it okay for different Reiki groups to have different ideas and rules? Why?

3. How do you know something is real? How would you prove to an alien from a planet with no love that love is real?

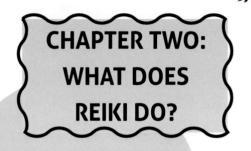

CHAPTER TWO: WHAT DOES REIKI DO?

All three have to be taken care of to be healthy and feel good. Doing things like brushing your teeth takes care of your body, and spending time reading (and not always watching television) takes care of your mind. Reiki is how you take care of your energy.

Reiki repairs your energy

So what does Reiki actually do? It repairs your energy. Actually, it repairs, relaxes and rebalances your energy.

The energy part of you gives you the strength and vitality to move and think. Have you ever been so tired you just

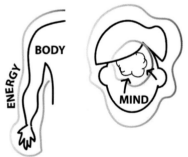

Did you know you're made of energy? You are. Everyone is. You have a body, a mind, and energy.

wanted to lie down and do nothing? Or noticed that your muscles feel weaker when you're ill? That's an example of your energy being very low, like an iPad running out of battery.

Your energy is also the reason you can sometimes feel someone is staring at you even when you can't see them, or you can feel someone close to you, even when they're not touching you. And it's okay if you've never felt that happen. If you start paying attention, you might start to feel it now, and many people start to feel their energy for the first time when they begin using Reiki. But even if you don't, you still have energy.

It's just that some people feel their energy more than others. It doesn't make anybody better or worse. It's just how we're built, like how some people are talented at art and some people are good at sports. But no matter how much you feel your energy, or don't feel it, you still have it, and you'll feel better when Reiki takes care of it.

People have spent years telling you how to take care of your body (do people still have to remind you to brush your teeth?). Perhaps you've been learning mindfulness in school to take care of your mind. But chances are that you haven't heard much about how to take care of your energy. This book is trying to fix that.

Reiki is how. Reiki is how you take care of the third part of you, your energy.

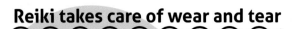

Reiki takes care of wear and tear

Reiki takes care of wear and tear. Wear and tear are not brother and sister bunny rabbits, although that would be a great name for a bunny rabbit superhero team, with capes and everything. "Wear and tear" is the expression used to describe what happens every day, to regular things, over time. It's like how things get dirty, just because they're there and being used.

Nobody came and poured a bucket of dirt on your shoes, but still, they get dirty and scuffed. Taking a pen to your shoes and drawing all over them is not wear and tear. Walking through a creek in them is not wear and tear. Both those things will damage your shoes, but they're not everyday, normal things.

It's the everyday normal damage that just happens because you're wearing your shoes and doing normal things: that's wear and tear. Everything gets dirty or damaged through wear and tear—your shoes, your hair, your t-shirts and your energy.

Your energy has to deal with wear and tear, just like everything in your life. It gets dirty and scuffed and maybe even a little ripped just by living your normal life. Life can be hard. School can be hard. Figuring out how to grow up and have friends, do good work, be nice when others are mean, and just live your life every day can be hard. Black and blue marks on your arms, scrapes on your knees, gunk on your teeth, and even small hurts in your heart, all these things are just the normal wear and tear of your everyday life.

Reiki is how you repair the way those things have affected your energy. You can't see the way your energy needs help because of the wear and tear on it, like you can with your black and blues or your shoes (hey, a friend just pointed out I made a rhyme. I'm a poet, and didn't even know it!), but it's still happening, and it still needs help. Reiki provides repair, rebalancing and relaxation to the wear and tear of everyday life on your energy so you can feel better.

ICYMI (In Case You Missed It, remember?)

Everything on this planet, absolutely everything, needs to be taken care of. If it's a person, an animal, a plant or a machine, it needs to be taken care of. Even sea cucumbers.

The reason we have to take care of things is because of wear and tear. Wear and tear is what we call the damage and dirtiness that happens to us and our possessions just because we are alive and do things every day.

But it's not enough to just take care of our body or our mind. We need to take care of the third part of us, our energy.

Not everybody knows we have energy. But the person who gave you this book does. And they want you to be able to take care of it just as well as the other things you take care of. The way you take care of your energy is with Reiki.

Reiki doesn't fix all things, but it does fix wear and tear. When you help repair your energy with Reiki, you will feel better and more relaxed.

Things to think about

1. Did you know all humans have energy before this book told you? When do you think people should learn about that?

2. What evidence do you have that energy exists other than this book? Do you feel your energy? What about other people's?

3. Do you think it matters that some people can feel energy more easily than others?

CHAPTER THREE: WHY IS REIKI IMPORTANT?

Because you are human

Why is Reiki important? Because you are human. Different species need to take care of themselves

differently, and you need to take care of yourself in human ways.

A cow may eat grass, but your human body would be very sick and feel terrible if you did that. A giraffe would have no clue what to do with a hairbrush, and a hamster will never need to take a shower.

Being a human means having to take care of yourself in human ways. Reiki is the human way of taking care of our energy.

Because without Reiki, things go wonky

If we don't take care of ourselves, trouble starts. It may not happen fast, but it always happens.

Let's pretend you

stopped taking care of your hair. No washing it, no brushing it. What would happen? At first it would just look messy. Maybe it would stick up in the back or stick out at your ears. Soon, you would start to get tangles and knots. The dirt and sweat that you stopped washing out with shampoo would stay there and get inside the tangles. This would make them bigger and hard when you touched them.

Eventually, all your hair would be like this, and it would start to hurt. It would pull on your head and it would hurt to lie down on it. Now what do you do? You can't brush it, and washing it won't help anymore. The only thing left to do is to cut off all your hair.

You could have a bald head (or very badly tangled, dirty hair, whichever you prefer). But when your new hair grew back, I bet you would never forget to take care of it again!

I'm sorry for what I said when I was hungry

Taking care of yourself can be incredibly annoying. But it's also the only way to make sure you feel good— and keep your hair! We need to make sure we get enough food, water and sleep. We need to make sure we feel safe and that we tell people what we think and feel. When these things don't happen, we usually feel badly in the same four ways: angry, sad, tired and/or worried. Maybe we don't feel these things all at once, and maybe we feel one or two of them more often than the others. But when a human doesn't give themselves good enough self-care, one, two, three or all four of those bad feelings will happen. We feel

angry, sad, tired and/or worried. But here's the great thing. If we're angry because we're hungry and we finally eat, we don't feel angry anymore. If we're tired because we haven't slept and we finally sleep, we don't feel tired anymore. And if we feel bad because we haven't done enough Reiki, we'll feel better as soon as we do!

There's a bunch of things human needs to stay okay: a home, rest, clean water, food, a place to feel safe, people who we love and who love us. Without them, we just don't do as well; things are harder. Reiki is part of that. We won't get sick without Reiki, like we would without water. But when we use it, we sleep better; we don't feel so bad, and we feel more relaxed. All of those things are good things to feel, and Reiki helps us do them.

ICYMI

You deserve to have a mouth that doesn't hurt and teeth that don't fall out. It's why people taught you to brush your teeth.

You also deserve to feel good. Not just okay, or a little better, but good and happy and peaceful.

To do that, you need to take care of all of you, your body, your mind AND your energy. You already know how to take care of your body and mind. Reiki is how humans take care of our energy, and that includes you.

I have no idea how sea cucumbers do it. But if you ever meet one, please ask them and let me know because I'm super curious.

Things to think about:

1. How do you know when it's time to take care of yourself, like eat, sleep or drink?

2. What happens to you and the people you know when you haven't gotten enough rest or enough food? How do you feel? How do they behave?

3. Which of the four things do you feel most when you need more self-care: angry, sad, tired, or worried?

4. Have you ever stopped taking care of yourself or something in your life? What happened?

5. Which do you think are the easiest and hardest pets to take care of? How do humans compare to that?

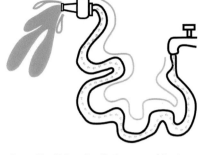

CHAPTER FOUR: HOW DOES REIKI WORK?

Where does Reiki come from?

Reiki comes from the planet the same way the water does. It's just here. When you give yourself Reiki, you'll be scooping it up, just like you scoop up air when you take a deep breath. It never goes away, it never runs out, and it never breaks.

How does Reiki get into my body?

Your teacher will make your body into a channel for Reiki. A "channel" is just another word for pipe or hose. The same way that water goes through a hose and comes out the other end, Reiki will go through you and out the other end, into your body. Your teacher will also teach you how to turn it on and off, and how to put it where you want it.

How does Reiki know where to go?

When you use your Reiki, it will come into your body and spread through you, going to all the places that need help, a little like the way water knows where to go. When you drink water, your body knows how to move the water from your mouth to your toes.

Reiki is the same. When you do your Reiki, it will spread through you and go into your energy, repairing the wear and tear that's happened during the day. As Reiki repairs things, your body will quickly be able to relax, and things will start to feel better.

Reiki can't do everything

Will Reiki make all the bad things go away? No. I'm sorry. Reiki can't do everything. Reiki is for the things that happen in your normal day-to-day life: things like falling off your bike, feeling nervous or finding it hard to sit still in class.

There are big things that happen to us sometimes, and Reiki may help a little, but not all the way. If you break your leg, you will need to go to the hospital. After you get out of the hospital and your leg hurts, your Reiki may help the pain feel a little better, and help put you to sleep. But Reiki won't fix it, and you'll still need a cast.

It's the same thing with bad feelings in your heart. Sometimes people are mean to us, or very sad things happen. Reiki will help us feel better, and that's so good, but it can't make all the bad feelings go away.

Reiki can't do everything. But it will do many, many things. And if you use it, you will feel better than you did before.

Remember, Reiki repairs, relaxes and rebalances your energy from the damage done by wear and tear during your day. Everything gets hurt from wear and tear: clothes, hair, shoes and your energy. You can't help your energy with a hairbrush, but you can use Reiki, and that is no small thing.

Reiki always works

Can you imagine if every time you drank water, you had to pay special attention to the water going into your body, or say a special thing in order for it to work? That would be SO annoying! Thankfully, we just drink. We drink while we watch a movie; we drink while we're listening to a friend; we drink while we eat; we drink and think about anything we want

while the water and our body just do their jobs. I'm drinking right now while I read what I've just written to see if there's any spelling mistakes!

Well, Reiki is the same. You don't have to think about anything special, do anything special or anything like that for Reiki to work. And you can do it while you're doing other things, just like drinking.

Also, you never have to worry about water breaking down and not making you wet (that would sure make swimming hard!), or the sun not making light. Reiki is the same at those things; it always works. Reiki just does its job, like air or water or light. Once your teacher teaches you how to do Reiki, it will never, ever break and it will always work. Always.

Even if you can't feel it, even if you haven't done it in a long time, even if you aren't sure. Reiki will work all the time, always. I find this very reassuring. Some days I feel Reiki more strongly than others, so it's a real relief to think that even when I don't feel it very strongly, it's still helping me just as much.

And to be honest, I have a tough time remembering

all the passwords, login names, and numbers I have for everything in my life already. (I still struggle with remembering how to convert fractions into decimal points.) I'm really glad I don't have to remember anything special or do anything special to get the help Reiki gives me.

I never have to worry if I'm doing it right or remember anything to make it happen. It just works. I wish everything was that easy!

Things to think about

1. How do you think your body knows how to move water to the right place?

2. What other things in your life always work no matter what, like Reiki? What things don't?

3. Reiki can't fix everything, do you know of something that CAN fix everything? What thing do you know about that fixes the most?

4. If water broke and didn't make you wet anymore, what would you want to swim in instead? What about showering?

CHAPTER FIVE: HOW DO YOU USE REIKI?

Find information and a teacher

To use Reiki, you need some information, which

you now have from this book. Well done—you've got the book you need! But you also need a teacher. I'm sorry I can't put a teacher inside this book. I hope a teacher gave you this book, because then you don't need anything else. But if they haven't, I would ask the adults around you to help you find one. Explain to them you think Reiki will help you, and you would like to try it. Maybe you can learn together? It would help them just as much as you, and it might be fun.

When you find your teacher

All teachers are a little different, but I will tell you what usually happens when people find their Reiki teacher. They will talk to you about Reiki and help you understand all about it. They will let you feel Reiki when they do it, so you can get used to what it feels like. You will be able to ask as many questions as you want. Teachers really like answering questions, but it's also okay if you don't have any. When you feel ready to learn for yourself, they will put you in a class. There will probably be other people your age learning as well, and you'll be able to meet them.

A Reiki class for young people usually takes two to four hours. Teachers usually start by giving you information—like the information in this book. When they get to the part where they show you how to do Reiki yourself, they will do something called an "attunement." If you said this word out loud syllable by syllable, it would sound like "ah-toon-ment." The attunement is the most special part of learning Reiki. Without it, nobody can do it, no matter how much they know about Reiki.

It also must be done with the student and teacher in the same room, which is why I can't give you an attunement while you read this book. This is the same reason why I can't give you a hug just by you reading this book, or over the phone or internet. We can talk about hugs, but to actually give you a hug, you and I have to be in the same place at the same time. Some things just need two people to be together. Giving a hug is one of them, and so is getting your Reiki attunement.

When I became a teacher, I promised my teacher I wouldn't tell anyone how to do the attunement unless they were learning to be a teacher themselves, so I can't tell you what actually happens during an attunement. But I can tell you it doesn't hurt. At all. In fact, it usually feels really cool. Also, it's not scary. Nothing shocking (or even fast) happens. Everything that happens is because you say it's okay, and you will be in control the whole time. And afterwards, you will be able to do Reiki and use it to make yourself feel better, which is super cool.

After the attunement part, you'll be able to do Reiki yourself, so most classes spend the rest of the time practicing. You'll practice on yourself, for sure. You'll also be able to practice doing it on others if you want to. When I teach young people, I really like having your parents come at the end of class so you can do it on them. It's so fun to see the adults' faces when you guys can do something so amazing and they have no idea how you did it!

And really, that's it. By the time the class ends, you'll know how to do Reiki, what to do while you're making it, where to put your hands, and how to make it stop. Most

importantly, it'll feel really normal and easy. By the time you leave, you'll feel confident and happy about what you're doing and ready to do it whenever you want to.

Reiki comes out of your hands

One of the things you'll learn in your class is that Reiki comes out of your hands. Honest, it really does! Once your teacher does your attunement, you will have Reiki come out of your hands when you want to, and stop it when you want to. That may sound like magic, but it isn't.

Many things feel like magic before you know how to do them. A little girl I know watched her daddy whistle and was completely convinced it was magic. Especially when he could whistle an actual song that she knew. She had no idea how her daddy did it; she had never seen anyone else do it, and when she put her lips in the same shape as her dad's, no sound came out. So, to her, of course it must be magic! But it wasn't. And eventually, with practice and her daddy teaching her, she could whistle herself. It wasn't magic; it was just something she hadn't learned how to do yet and couldn't imagine how anyone else was doing it.

Reiki is the same. It may sound like magic now, but very quickly Reiki will feel very normal and very easy. And it's SO much easier than learning to whistle.

Learning to whistle takes days or weeks to learn, and months before you're really good at it. When your teacher shows you how to do Reiki, you'll be able to do it in a few minutes. Yep, a few minutes. That's how easy it is to do Reiki once you've got your teacher and take your class.

How to turn Reiki on and off

So now you have your book, your teacher, and your Reiki in your hands. What happens next? Well, all you have to do is put your hand in a cupped position and put it on your body. If you don't know what a cupped hand position is, do this: take your hand and put it on your shoulder. Do you see how your hand is now curved? Almost like a C shape? That is a cupped position. You can use one hand or both, whichever you prefer.

If you left your hand there on your shoulder, it would start putting Reiki into your shoulder. If you moved your cupped hand to your knee, your hand would start putting Reiki into your knee. If you put your hand on your belly, you would start to put Reiki into your belly. That's it. You put your hand into that cupped, round position and put it on your body. It doesn't even have to touch you, your hand just has to be near your body and pointing towards it. As soon as you do that, you are using Reiki. And it doesn't matter where you put your hand, put it wherever you want.

Remember, your body will move the Reiki wherever it wants it to go, just like drinking water. Water goes into your mouth, and your body knows how to move it to your toes.

Reiki does, too. Easy, peasy, lemon squeezy.

When you want to stop using Reiki, just stop making your hand cupped and let it relax. You could make your hand flat, straight, or you could spread your fingers. It doesn't matter. As soon as you stop making your hand into that cupped shape, Reiki stops. You start it and stop it by changing the shape of your hand. You control if you want it on or off

If you forget what you're supposed to do with your hand, just put it back on your shoulder or the top of your head. That is the right shape to turn Reiki on. Then take your hand and put it anywhere you want. When you do this, Reiki will go into your body and help you feel better. And when you're done, just put your hand in any regular position.

To turn Reiki on, put your hand in the cupped position and put it on or above your body. It doesn't matter where or how long you leave it there. To turn Reiki off, put your hand in any other shape you want.

Don't twist your pipe

Do you remember I said that when you learn to do Reiki you'll be a channel, which is sorta like becoming a hose or pipe that Reiki can flow out of? Well, if you twist a hose, less water will come out of it, and it's the same with Reiki. If you cross your arms or legs, you'll find less Reiki flows out of you.

One or two hands

Reiki works if you want to use both hands or just one. You get to decide what feels best for you. You may find that you like doing one hand sometimes and both hands sometimes. I like doing Reiki while I read, so I often hold my book with one hand and do Reiki with the other. But I also like watching TV while I do my Reiki. When I do that, I watch TV and put both my cupped hands on my lap. You get to decide when you do your Reiki and how you do your Reiki. The only thing you have to do is have one or both of your hands cupped when you do it.

You can do it while you do other things

You can't talk when you brush your teeth. (Well, not very well anyway!) You can't do your homework while you take a shower, and you can't ride your bike when you wash your clothes. But as long as your hand is cupped, you can do Reiki while you do anything else.

Most people feel Reiki more when they're sitting quietly to do it, and that might be true of you, too. But that doesn't mean it's working any better. It just means you can feel it better because you're not paying attention to other things and can really pay attention to the feeling of Reiki.

I really love sitting down quietly, closing my eyes and feeling my Reiki. I have a swinging chair in my backyard, and it's a great place to be alone, relax and feel Reiki. I like doing it at night too, before I go to sleep. I like to lie in bed and do Reiki and let everything slow down until I drift off to sleep. I rest my hands on my belly, so it's easy to fall asleep that way. Those are the times I feel Reiki the most, and it's a very cool feeling.

But during the day I have things to do, just like you. And there's usually a lot of people around me, and I don't always want people to know that I'm doing Reiki. But I still want to feel better! That's why it's so great that we can do Reiki while we do other things. I've already told you I do Reiki when I watch TV, sitting on my couch. I also do it while I do all kinds of things, like stand in line, eat my lunch, ride in the car, and when I talk to people. I don't feel it as much as I do when I'm sitting quietly, but it still works just as well, so it helps me feel better just as much. It's nice to have that special quiet time with Reiki, but it's really great that it still works even when I can't feel it as much because I'm doing other things. And I LOVE that I can do it when I feel bad during the day and it'll help me feel better.

Nobody else will notice

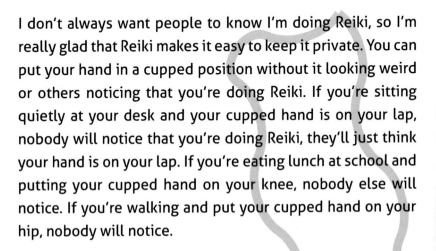

I don't always want people to know I'm doing Reiki, so I'm really glad that Reiki makes it easy to keep it private. You can put your hand in a cupped position without it looking weird or others noticing that you're doing Reiki. If you're sitting quietly at your desk and your cupped hand is on your lap, nobody will notice that you're doing Reiki, they'll just think your hand is on your lap. If you're eating lunch at school and putting your cupped hand on your knee, nobody else will notice. If you're walking and put your cupped hand on your hip, nobody will notice.

You can do Reiki whenever you want and nobody else

will notice. When you're taking a test, when you're giving a presentation at school, when you're talking to someone that makes you nervous, when you're angry and trying not to yell or get in trouble—any time you want. Remember, it doesn't matter what you're thinking about or where you are, you just need one or two hands in a cupped position near or on your body. Oh, and try not to cross your feet or arms, so your channel is  open and not kinked up. You can use it to help you feel more relaxed and calmer whenever you want and keep it totally private at the same time. I love that about Reiki.

The more you do, the stronger your Reiki gets

For most people, they feel Reiki the more they do it. At first, it's unfamiliar and may be hard to know how to explain what it feels like. It's a new thing, and it takes time to get comfortable and feel confident with it. That is not a problem, and it's true for almost everyone, even adults. (Actually, it's especially true of adults. In my experience, adults take more time than younger people with most of this. That's why when

I have classes for younger people, they're two to four hours, but for adults, they're six to eight hours! You guys just feel things more easily and talk about it more easily. Sssssh ... don't tell them!) Anyway, it's probable that the more you do Reiki, the more you'll feel, and the easier it'll be to find words to explain it.

Also, the more you do Reiki the stronger it will get, like a muscle. The more you use it, the stronger it gets, and so will the energy in your body. This is true for everyone, even people who don't feel it so strongly. This is a little like a plant that hasn't been getting enough water. It'll start dry and droopy, and maybe the leaves will be brown. The first day you water it, it'll feel better. The second day, even better. If you keep watering it and giving it what it needs, in one month it'll have bright green leaves and be full of life. Reiki is the same. Every day you do Reiki, your energy will get stronger and stronger, and over time, you'll feel better and better.

ICYMI

I've given you lots and lots of information about how Reiki works, but all you really have to remember is how easy it is.

- You don't need a special place, you can do it anywhere.

- You don't need special words or special thoughts.

- You can use one hand or two.

- You can do it while you're doing other things, like watching TV, eating your lunch, or reading a book.

- To turn it on, put your hand in a round, cupped, position that looks like the letter "C" and put it on, or pointing towards, your body.

- To turn it off, put your hand in any other position.

- If you cross your arms or legs, it'll flow out of you slower, but it'll still work.

- The more you do it, the stronger it'll get, even if you don't feel it that much.

- You can keep it private if you want to.

Reiki is super easy to do, and yet, it will help you feel SO much better.

Things to think about

1. I promised my teacher not to tell anyone details about an attunement unless they were becoming a Reiki teacher. Do you think that's fair? Why or why not? Why do you think my teacher asked me to make that promise?

2. What things have you learned that look like magic, or really hard to other people, but are easy for you? Were they always easy for you?

3. Which part of our body do you think you'll use to help you remember the cupped hand position?

4. Why do you think it's sometimes harder for adults to feel Reiki or explain what they feel? How would you help them?

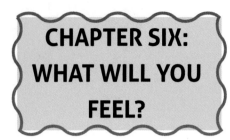

CHAPTER SIX: WHAT WILL YOU FEEL?

Everyone is different

Everyone's body is different, that's why some of us prefer vanilla ice cream and some of us prefer chocolate. Some people don't like ice cream at all (although that's still hard for me to believe)! This means that everyone feels Reiki a little differently, and so I can't tell you what it'll feel like for you. But I can give you some clues to look for based on what others have felt.

Lots of people feel Reiki as heat. Lots of people say they feel tingling, and lots of people say they feel floaty and lighter. I've also heard some people say Reiki feels cold to them, and that it feels heavy. Do you see what I mean about how it's different for everyone? I've never met anybody who said it had a smell, but I wouldn't be surprised if I did some

There are no normal people, there are just different kinds of weird!

day. Everyone really is different. People often want to know what others do or feel so they can know if they're normal or okay. But with Reiki,

you get to know and feel what you feel, because it's your body that's doing the feeling, no one else's. There is no normal, there's just what you feel.

It's the same with where people feel their Reiki. Some people feel it in their hands, some people feel it in their bodies, and some people aren't really sure where they feel it or if they feel it at all. If you ask those people to try really hard to describe it, they'll often say it's sort of everywhere and nowhere at the same time, which of course makes no sense unless you're the person feeling that!

And remember, not everyone feels energy anyway. And that doesn't make any difference at all to how much Reiki works. Have you ever had a cold and not been able to smell or taste anything? The food takes up space in your mouth, but there's no taste at all, even when you swallow. The thing is, even when you can't taste anything, the food still does its job. You may not taste or smell the food because of your cold, but as soon as that food gets to your belly, you'll begin to feel less hungry, you'll start to feel more settled and relaxed, and the process of giving your body the nutrition it needs has begun. Reiki can be the same. You may feel your Reiki (or taste the food), but even when you can't, the food and the Reiki are still helping you feel better and giving your body what it needs.

The point is, there's no way to get it wrong, it's just what you feel ... or not. Regardless of what you do or don't

feel, Reiki will always work and will always do its job of repairing the wear and tear in your energy to help you feel calmer and more relaxed. In that way, Reiki is very simple.

How your body feels is more important

Feeling how your body feels because you're doing Reiki is more important than feeling the Reiki energy in your hand. Knowing how your body feels when you do your Reiki is part of knowing who you are, and that's how you learn to take care of yourself.

When people feel Reiki, they can often feel their body begin to relax. That means their breathing slows down, their shoulders slide down their backs, even their face gets softer. Some people feel pain in their body go away, and some people say they just "feel better," even though it's hard to talk about or explain. Many people take a deep breath and then start to breath more easily. Some people feel less worried, or nervous, or that it's easier for them to be patient. I've heard from many people that everyone around them is less annoying when they do their Reiki (especially younger siblings!). But the whole world hasn't changed, it's just the people doing Reiki who are more patient. All of these things, and anything else, are correct and OK.

ICYMI

Every human I've ever met (me too) wonders if we are normal. It's such a normal thing to do, it should prove to all of us how normal we really are! We want to be part of things and belong. So we compare if what we're doing is what everyone else is doing or if they (who is this "They" person anyway, and why do they get to decide?!) is going to kick us out because we're different.

This is especially true when we are trying new things that we're unsure of, and that includes Reiki.

Truth is, though, nobody is exactly alike, not even what people call "identical twins." If you've ever known a pair, you know that when you get to know them you can tell them apart easily.

You will feel Reiki how you feel it because you are you. It will be a little the same, and a little different, than everyone else who has ever felt.....or not felt...their Reiki.

THIS IS TRUE OF EVERYONE.

So do your best (you won't be perfect) to feeeeeeeeeeeeeeeeeeel what YOU feeeeeeeeeeeeeeeeeeel when you do YOUR Reiki.

Things to think about:

1. Why do you think humans worry about being normal, but dogs and sea cucumbers don't?

2. What is your hypothesis for why some people like vanilla and some people like chocolate? Do you think it's the same reason different people feel Reiki differently?

3. When you eat something, what do you feel or taste in your mouth? What do you feel in your body? Do you think one is more important than the other?

4. Why do you think knowing how you feel helps you take care of yourself?

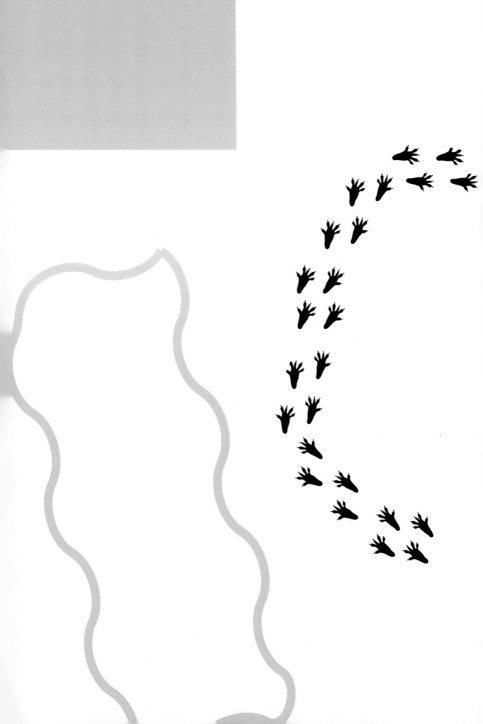

CHAPTER SEVEN: WHEN SHOULD YOU USE YOUR REIKI?

How often and for how long?

Your body would like a little bit of Reiki every day. There are things that you do once and you never have to do them again, like being born, or learning

how to ride a bike. But most things we need to do over and over again, like eating or sleeping. We also can't sleep a lot on Monday and hope it'll help us on Friday! Reiki is like that. Humans need a little bit of Reiki every day, and doing lots today doesn't mean you won't need any tomorrow.

You don't need a lot, though. Most people your age only need about ten minutes (adults need twenty minutes). You don't have to do it all at the same time, either. You can if you want to, but you can also do a little bit every once in a while. I know people who like to do a little in the morning, a little later and a little at bedtime. I also know people who like to do all of it at once in the car on the way to school. It really doesn't matter. You can do Reiki whenever you want, you get to decide. Just use it every day with a cupped hand.

When?

The other great thing about Reiki is that you don't have to sit and do it like you have to sit down and do your homework. You can do Reiki whenever you want, with one or two hands, and you can do it for a few seconds or a few minutes. Whatever you do, Reiki always works.

I do Reiki when I bump my knee. I do Reiki when I'm watching television. I do Reiki when my stomach hurts. I do Reiki at bedtime. I do Reiki when I'm listening to boring people talk and I'm having trouble sitting still. (Yes, that happens for adults, too. Adult meetings can be incredibly boring sometimes, UGH.)

The important thing is, it's up to you when you do it, how long you do it, and if you want to tell anyone about it. Just do it, every day. All you have to do is put one or both hands in a cupped position and put it anywhere on your body. And remember, one of the great things about Reiki is that when you do it, nobody has to know that you're doing anything. They won't see it. They may notice that you feel better if they're paying attention, but they won't know why. You can always tell them about it if you want to, but you don't have to.

ICYMI

You are a young person, so I bet you wish you had more control over things. Like when you go to sleep, how much you get to be on devices like iPads or TV, how much sugar you can eat in one day, and all the other ways that other people tell you what to do, when to do it and how to do it. Reiki is different. It is something that is all yours.

- You can do it anytime you want.

- You can do it however you want.

- You can do it as long as you want.

Reiki is going to make you feel better and it's yours to use for just that. Nobody else has to know or decide for you.

Most young people tell me that adults don't understand how hard it is to be a young person, even though they say they do. So you use your Reiki to help you deal with it all.

Things to think about:

1. You do some things every day and some things just once. Which of them do you prefer?

2. Do you think you'll do your Reiki all in one go or a few times during the day? Why?

3. Why do you think adults need to do twenty minutes of Reiki a day, but people your age only need ten?

4. Why do you feel most adults seem to forget how hard it is to be your age? Do you think that will happen to you? Why and Why not?

CHAPTER EIGHT:
IN THEIR OWN WORDS

Here are things that other young people have said about Reiki:

"Reiki tingles, it feels really cool."

"We do mindfulness at school, and I always do my Reiki then. It helps my body feel soft."

"I thought the walls were grey, but after my attunement they looked green!"

"I like doing Reiki on my friends when they hurt themselves."

"Why did you write this WHOLE book! Just tell them to do it, it's really easy and awesome."

"Reiki feels gooey."

"My dad always asks me to do Reiki on him because it helps his back feel better."

"I have test anxiety and my tutor suggested I learn Reiki. I use it before and during tests and it helps me calm down."

"I always do Reiki in bed. I sleep soooooooooo much better."

"My friend said she didn't believe in Reiki. Whatever. I told her that's like not believing in water."

"Reiki's kinda crazy, but I really love it. It also makes my little brother seem a lot less annoying."

CONCLUSION

Phew! That was a lot of information, huh?! Here, stare at a hedgehog for a bit, just for fun.

Does it feel weird to find out that you are made up of a body, a mind AND energy after all these years? And that Reiki exists and can do all these great things? If someone had told you this earlier, it certainly would have made your life much easier. Less pain, less stress, and less bad feelings. You would have had something you could have done to help yourself feel better.

The thing is, the adults around you probably didn't know until recently, and they've probably been looking for a way to let you know, too. I didn't find out about Reiki until I was eighteen, and most people think that's really early. (By the way, some adults don't even know about it now, which always makes me a little sad, as they're missing out on so much.) So while it may seem late for you, a lot of adults will be impressed (and maybe a little jealous) that you've learned so early in your life.

But now you know, and you'll never not know again. I hope this book helps you understand a little bit more about how you and your energy works, how to use Reiki to help you feel better, and how you can take a little bit more control over your life by using it. And although you still need a teacher to help you have Reiki in your hands—that won't be a hard thing to find. And once you've got that, you've got everything you need. Really. If you forgot everything you've read here, it wouldn't really matter. (But do remember the hedgehogs, hedgehogs are great.) The only thing that matters is that you put your hand in a cupped position and give yourself Reiki, a little every day.

I like taking about Reiki, and I've really enjoyed writing this for you. I can't think of anything else that you need to know. Now it is up to you. You will need to decide what you do next. I hope you do things that help you have a good life and to feel as good as you possibly can.

I believe Reiki will help you do that. It is a big help to me, my family, my friends, and to many, many other people all over the world. You will have a great time, learn lots and always have a way to help yourself feel better. You deserve that. Good luck and enjoy all of it!

ABOUT THE AUTHOR

Tiffany was born in New York City. She first learned that humans have energy when she was eighteen years old, and it changed how she saw everything in her life. Thirty-five years later, she's still amazed by how much there is to learn. She lived in London and went to school there for a long time. It means she gets to put letters after her name now, which impresses some adults. But even better, she got to see hedgehogs there all the time. They lived in her back garden! (That's what people there call their backyards.)

She lives in California now and created an energy medicine health clinic that uses energy vibrations like Reiki to help people feel happier and healthier. It's called Healing for People (www.HealingforPeople.com), and they offer individual healing sessions and classes for young people and adults. She moved to California twenty years ago, and she still thinks it's weird that the Golden Gate Bridge isn't gold. And she misses the hedgehogs.

Made in the USA
Las Vegas, NV
02 December 2021

35859721R00045